Introduction

Winnie the Pooh is a beloved character in children's literature and popular culture. Created by author A.A. Milne in 1926, Winnie the Pooh is a friendly and kindhearted bear who lives in the Hundred Acre Wood with his friends Piglet, Tigger, Eeyore, Rabbit, Kanga, Roo, and Owl. The stories featuring Winnie the Pooh and his friends have been translated into multiple languages and have been adapted into various forms of media, including films, television shows, and merchandise.

Winnie the Pooh's significance in popular culture lies in the timeless messages of friendship, perseverance, mindfulness, kindness, and imagination that his stories convey. Through his adventures in the Hundred Acre Wood, Winnie the Pooh teaches children and adults alike valuable life lessons and provides a source of comfort and joy. Winnie the Pooh's popularity has endured for almost a century and continues to be a cherished character in the hearts of many.

Purpose of This Book

I hope that you'll find inspiration in these pages, exploring the timeless wisdom found in Winnie the Pooh's quotes. It can be a fun and enriching experience for readers of all ages and here are some ways to do so:

Read the original books: A.A. Milne's original Winnie the Pooh books are a treasure trove of quotes that showcase the wisdom and humor of the characters. Reading the books in their entirety can provide a deeper understanding of the messages that the characters convey.

Reflect on the quotes: Choose some of your favorite Winnie the Pooh quotes and reflect on what they mean to you. Consider how they relate to your own life and experiences.

Apply the quotes to everyday situations: Look for opportunities to apply the lessons from Winnie the Pooh's quotes to everyday situations. For example, if you come across a challenging situation, reflect on how Winnie the Pooh and his friends would approach it and try to apply their wisdom to your own situation.

Discuss the quotes with others: Engage in conversations with others about the wisdom found in Winnie the Pooh's quotes. Discuss how they have impacted your life and how you can apply them to your everyday experiences.

Create art or crafts inspired by the quotes: Get creative and make art or crafts inspired by your favorite Winnie the Pooh quotes. This can be a fun way to explore the quotes and express your own creativity.

Overall, exploring the timeless wisdom found in Winnie the Pooh's quotes can be a rewarding and enriching experience that can help readers to find greater meaning and purpose in their everyday lives.

As you read this small book of quotes, take the time to let Pooh's words sink in and truly change your life for the better.

POOH QUOTES

Pooh Quotes

THE ART OF DOING NOTHING: LESSONS FROM WINNIE THE POOH

Matt Hobbs

A. A. Milne

Hobbs Publishing

Contents

Introduction   i

1   Friendship   1

2   Friendship   3

3   Friendship   4

4   Friendship   5

5   Friendship   6

6   Friendship   7

7   Friendship   8

8   Friendship   9

9   Friendship   10

10   Friendship   11

11   Friendship   12

12   Friendship   13

13   Friendship   14

14   Friendship   15

15	Friendship	16
16	Friendship	17
17	Friendship	18
18	Perseverance	19
19	Perseverance	21
20	Perseverance	22
21	Perseverance	23
22	Perseverance	24
23	Perseverance	25
24	Perseverance	26
25	Perseverance	27
26	Perseverance	28
27	Perseverance	29
28	Perseverance	30
29	Perseverance	31
30	Perseverance	32
31	Perseverance	33
32	Perseverance	34
33	Mindfulness	35
34	Mindfulness	37
35	Mindfulness	38

36	Mindfulness	39
37	Mindfulness	40
38	Mindfulness	41
39	Mindfulness	42
40	Mindfulness	43
41	Mindfulness	44
42	Mindfulness	45
43	Mindfulness	46
44	Kindness	47
45	Kindness	49
46	Kindness	50
47	Kindness	51
48	Kindness	52
49	Kindness	53
50	Kindness	54
51	Kindness	55
52	Kindness	56
53	Kindness	57
54	Imagination	58
55	Imagination	60
56	Imagination	61

57	Imagination	62
58	Imagination	63
59	Imagination	64
60	Imagination	65
61	Imagination	66
62	Imagination	67
63	Imagination	68
64	Imagination	69
65	Imagination	70
66	Imagination	71
67	Imagination	72
68	Conclusion	73

Note from the Author 75

1

Friendship

Quotes from Winnie the Pooh and his friends that highlight the importance of Friendship.

As Winnie the Pooh once said, "A day without a friend is like a pot without honey." Friendship is incredibly important, not just to Pooh but to all of us. Here are a few reasons why:

1. Companionship: Friends provide us with companionship, someone to share our experiences with, both good and bad. Having a friend means you're never alone, and that can be a great comfort.
2. Support: Friends are there to support us when we

need it most. They can offer advice, lend a listening ear, or simply be a shoulder to cry on.
3. Fun: Friends make life more enjoyable! Whether it's going on an adventure, sharing a laugh, or simply enjoying each other's company, friends bring joy into our lives.
4. Growth: Friends help us grow and learn. They challenge us to be our best selves, and they can provide valuable feedback and encouragement along the way.

Overall, friendship is a vital component of a happy and fulfilling life. As Winnie the Pooh reminds us, "You can't stay in your corner of the Forest waiting for others to come to you. You have to go to them sometimes." So let these quotes be your inspiration to go out and make some friends!

2

Friendship

"We'll be friends until forever, just you wait and see."

3

Friendship

"You can't stay in your corner of the forest waiting for others to come to you. You have to go to them sometimes."

4

Friendship

"Sometimes the smallest things take up the most room in your heart."

5

Friendship

"How lucky I am to have something that makes saying goodbye so hard."

6

Friendship

"If there ever comes a day when we can't be together, keep me in your heart, I'll stay there forever."

7

Friendship

"It's not what we have, but who we have."

8

Friendship

"Some people care too much. I think it's called love."

9

Friendship

"You can't help respecting anybody who can spell TUESDAY, even if he doesn't spell it right."

10

Friendship

"It is more fun to talk with someone who doesn't use long, difficult words but rather short, easy words like 'What about lunch?'"

11

Friendship

"It's so much more friendly with two."

12

Friendship

"We didn't realize we were making memories, we just knew we were having fun."

13

Friendship

"If you live to be a hundred, I hope I live to be a hundred minus one day, so I never have to live without you."

14

Friendship

"I think we dream so we don't have to be apart for so long. If we're in each other's dreams, we can be together all the time."

15

Friendship

"As soon as I saw you, I knew an adventure was going to happen."

16

Friendship

"You don't spell it... you feel it."
(about friendship)

17

Friendship

***

The previous quotes showcase the enduring bond of friendship between the characters in the Hundred Acre Wood and the importance of having good friends in our lives.

18

Perseverance

Quotes from Winnie the Pooh and his friends that highlight the importance of Perseverance.

Winnie the Pooh once said, "Rivers know this: there is no hurry. We shall get there some day." This quote embodies the importance of perseverance, or the ability to persist in the face of difficulty. Here are a few reasons why perseverance is so important, from the voice of Winnie the Pooh:

1. Overcoming obstacles: Life is full of obstacles, but with perseverance, we can overcome them. Whether it's a challenging project at work, a difficult personal

goal, or simply getting through a tough day, perseverance can help us push through and succeed.
2. Learning and growth: Perseverance can help us learn and grow. When we persist through challenges, we develop new skills, gain new insights, and become more resilient.
3. Achieving our dreams: Perseverance is often the key to achieving our dreams. Whether it's starting a new business, writing a book, or pursuing a passion, perseverance helps us stay focused and committed even when the going gets tough.
4. Building character: Perseverance can help us build character and become the best version of ourselves. By persevering through challenges, we develop qualities like resilience, determination, and courage.

Overall, perseverance is a powerful tool for achieving our goals and becoming the best version of ourselves. As Winnie the Pooh said, "When life throws you a rainy day, play in the puddles." So when the going gets tough, remember to keep pushing forward, because success is often just around the corner.

19

Perseverance

"Rivers know this: there is no hurry. We shall get there some day."

20

Perseverance

"When you are a Bear of Very Little Brain, and you Think of Things, you find sometimes that a Thing which seemed very Thingish inside you is quite different when it gets out into the open and has other people looking at it."

21

Perseverance

"I am not lost, for I know where I am. But however, where I am may be lost."

22

Perseverance

"The things that make me different are the things that make me, me."

23

Perseverance

"I always get to where I'm going by walking away from where I have been."

24

Perseverance

"I used to believe in forever, but forever's too good to be true."

25

Perseverance

"I'm not lost for I know where I am going. But it's just that where I am going, the way is a little unclear."

26

Perseverance

"You are braver than you believe, stronger than you seem, and smarter than you think."

27

Perseverance

"I wasn't going to eat it. I was just going to taste it."

28

Perseverance

"You can't help someone get up a hill without getting closer to the top yourself."

29

Perseverance

"I'm just a bear, sitting here, minding my own business, waiting for somebody to love me."

30

Perseverance

"It never hurts to keep looking for sunshine."

31

Perseverance

"The nicest thing about the rain is that it always stops. Eventually."

32

Perseverance

***

The previous quotes showcase the importance of perseverance and determination, even when the path ahead may seem uncertain or difficult. They encourage us to keep moving forward, to believe in ourselves and to take comfort in the simple pleasures of life.

33

Mindfulness

Quotes from Winnie the Pooh and his friends that highlight the importance of Mindfulness.

Winnie the Pooh once said, "Don't underestimate the value of doing nothing, of just going along, listening to all the things you can't hear, and not bothering." This quote embodies the importance of mindfulness, or the practice of being present in the moment and aware of our thoughts and feelings. Here are a few reasons why mindfulness is so important, from the voice of Winnie the Pooh:

1. Reducing stress: Mindfulness can help reduce stress by allowing us to focus on the present moment rather

than worrying about the future or dwelling on the past. By staying present, we can cultivate a sense of calm and tranquility.
2. Improving focus: Mindfulness can also help improve focus and concentration. By training our minds to stay present, we can become more attentive and focused on the task at hand.
3. Enhancing relationships: Mindfulness can improve our relationships by helping us become more aware of our thoughts, feelings, and reactions. By being mindful in our interactions with others, we can communicate more effectively and cultivate deeper connections.
4. Increasing happiness: Mindfulness can also increase our sense of happiness and well-being. By staying present and appreciating the little things in life, we can cultivate a sense of gratitude and joy.

Overall, mindfulness is a powerful tool for reducing stress, improving focus, enhancing relationships, and increasing happiness. As Winnie the Pooh said, "Sometimes the smallest things take up the most room in your heart." So take some time to be present and appreciate the little things in life, because they can bring us great joy and fulfillment.

34

Mindfulness

"Think, think, think."

35

Mindfulness

"Doing nothing often leads to the very best kind of something."

36

Mindfulness

"I think we dream so we don't have to be apart for so long. If we're in each other's dreams, we can be together all the time."

37

Mindfulness

"Sometimes, if you stand on the bottom rail of a bridge and lean over to watch the river slipping slowly away beneath you, you will suddenly know everything there is to be known."

38

Mindfulness

"Don't underestimate the value of doing nothing, of just going along, listening to all the things you can't hear, and not bothering."

39

Mindfulness

"Weeds are flowers, too, once you get to know them."

40

Mindfulness

"The most important thing is, even when we're apart... I'll always be with you."

41

Mindfulness

"A little consideration, a little thought for others, makes all the difference."

42

Mindfulness

"I used to believe in forever, but forever's too good to be true."

43

Mindfulness

***

The previous quotes encourage us to slow down, be present in the moment, and appreciate the simple joys of life. They remind us to take a break from our busy lives and spend time with the people we care about, and to be kind and considerate towards others. They also emphasize the importance of self-reflection and personal growth, and encourage us to believe in ourselves and our abilities.

44

Kindness

Quotes from Winnie the Pooh and his friends that highlight the importance of Kindness.

Winnie the Pooh once said, "A little consideration, a little thought for others, makes all the difference." This quote embodies the importance of kindness, or the act of showing compassion and understanding to others. Here are a few reasons why kindness is so important, from the voice of Winnie the Pooh:

1. Spreading positivity: Kindness can spread positivity and create a ripple effect. When we show kindness to others, it can inspire them to show kindness to others

as well, creating a chain reaction of positivity and compassion.
2. Building relationships: Kindness can also help us build stronger relationships with others. By showing kindness and empathy, we can create deeper connections and foster a sense of trust and understanding.
3. Improving mental health: Kindness can also improve our own mental health by boosting our mood and reducing stress. When we show kindness to others, it can also create a sense of purpose and fulfillment, which can improve our overall well-being.
4. Making a difference: Kindness can make a real difference in the world. Even small acts of kindness, like holding the door open for someone or offering a kind word, can have a positive impact on someone's day and even their life.

Overall, kindness is a powerful tool for creating positivity, building relationships, improving mental health, and making a difference in the world. As Winnie the Pooh said, "Some people care too much, I think it's called love." So let's all strive to show a little more kindness, compassion, and love to those around us.

45

Kindness

"A day without a friend is like a pot without a single drop of honey left inside."

46

Kindness

"A little consideration, a little thought for others, makes all the difference."

47

Kindness

"It's always useful to know where a friend-and-relation is, whether you want him or whether you don't."

48

Kindness

"Nobody can be uncheered with a balloon."

49

Kindness

"Sometimes the smallest things take up the most room in your heart."

50

Kindness

"How do you spell love?" - "You don't spell it... you feel it."

51

Kindness

"If the person you are talking to doesn't appear to be listening, be patient. It may simply be that he has a small piece of fluff in his ear."

52

Kindness

"You can't help someone get up a hill without getting closer to the top yourself."

53

Kindness

* * *

The previous quotes emphasize the importance of kindness, empathy, and understanding towards others. They encourage us to be patient, considerate, and to appreciate the unique qualities and differences of ourselves and others. They also emphasize the importance of friendship and connection, and remind us to never give up hope, even during difficult times.

54

Imagination

Quotes from Winnie the Pooh and his friends that highlight the importance of Imagination.

Winnie the Pooh once said, "I'm not just a bear, I'm a Pooh. And that means I'm smarter than the average bear." This quote embodies the importance of imagination, or the ability to think creatively and envision new possibilities. Here are a few reasons why imagination is so important, from the voice of Winnie the Pooh:

1. Fostering creativity: Imagination is essential for fostering creativity. When we imagine new possibilities

and envision different outcomes, we can come up with innovative ideas and solutions.
2. Developing problem-solving skills: Imagination can also help us develop problem-solving skills. By thinking creatively and outside the box, we can approach problems in new and different ways.
3. Encouraging learning: Imagination can encourage learning by making it more engaging and enjoyable. When we imagine different scenarios and possibilities, we can better understand concepts and retain information.
4. Enhancing play: Imagination can enhance play by making it more fun and immersive. When we use our imagination to create new games and activities, we can turn even the most mundane tasks into something enjoyable.

Overall, imagination is a powerful tool for fostering creativity, developing problem-solving skills, encouraging learning, and enhancing play. As Winnie the Pooh said, "Think, think, think." So let's all take a moment to use our imaginations and explore new possibilities, because you never know what new and exciting things you might discover.

55

Imagination

"Imagination is more important than knowledge."

56

Imagination

"A little fantasy goes a long way."

57

Imagination

"I'm not lost for I know where I am going. But it's just that where I am going, the way is a little unclear."

58

Imagination

"I like the thought of me best."

59

Imagination

"When life throws you a rainy day, play in the puddles."

60

Imagination

"Think it over, think it under."

61

Imagination

"The moment where you doubt whether you can fly, you cease forever being able to do it."

62

Imagination

"I'm never lost for long, because there's always something to find."

63

Imagination

"I'm not good at the advice. Can I interest you in a sarcastic comment?"

64

Imagination

"People who don't think probably don't have brains; rather, they have grey fluff that's blown into their heads by mistake."

65

Imagination

"I'm not really a person who likes to tell anyone how to live, but it is your life, and I would like to see you live it well."

66

Imagination

"A little nonsense now and then is relished by the wisest men."

67

Imagination

***

The previous quotes highlight the importance of imagination, creativity, and adventure. They encourage us to step out of our comfort zones and embrace new experiences, and to never stop dreaming and exploring. They also remind us to appreciate the simple things in life and find joy in the little moments.

68

Conclusion

Throughout the collection of Winnie the Pooh quotes, several themes and lessons emerge that are relevant to our lives. These include the importance of friendship, perseverance, mindfulness, kindness, imagination, and the value of simplicity.

The quotes about friendship emphasize the importance of being there for one another and cherishing the people in our lives. The quotes about perseverance remind us to keep pushing forward, even in difficult times. The quotes about mindfulness encourage us to be present and enjoy the moment, and to focus on what really matters in life. The quotes about kindness remind us to treat others with compassion and empathy. The quotes about imagination encourage us to explore new ideas and experiences, and to never stop dreaming.

Ultimately, the enduring wisdom of Winnie the Pooh and his quotes lies in the simplicity and universality. They are applicable to people of all ages and backgrounds, and can provide comfort, inspiration, and guidance in many different situations.

Whether we're dealing with challenges, celebrating achievements, or simply trying to navigate the ups and downs of daily life, there's a Winnie the Pooh quote that can offer insight and wisdom. The enduring popularity of these quotes is a testament to their power and relevance, and serves as a reminder that sometimes the simplest words can have the greatest impact.

Note from the Author

Let me tell you, Winnie the Pooh and his friends have some serious wisdom. I mean, who would have thought that a little bear and his buddies could teach us so much about life?

From the importance of friendship, perseverance, and kindness to the power of imagination, mindfulness, and simplicity, these characters have so much to offer. And the best part is that their messages are timeless. They apply just as much today as they did when they were first written.

So, if you're feeling lost or overwhelmed, take a page from Winnie the Pooh's book and slow down. Take a moment to appreciate the world around you, spend time with loved ones, and focus on the things that matter most.

And always remember, in the words of Winnie the Pooh himself, "You're braver than you believe, and stronger than you seem, and smarter than you think."

All the Best,
-Matt Hobbs

Milton Keynes UK
Ingram Content Group UK Ltd.
UKHW030105141223
434291UK00016B/1038